D0464841

# Hula

DAVEY

Hawaiian Proverbs and Inspirational Quotes Celebrating Hula in Hawai'i

Mutual Publishing

Library of Congress Catalog Card Number: 2003111998
ISBN 1-56647-638-0

Design by Mardee Domingo Melton

First Printing, November 2003

Mutual Publishing, LLC
1215 Center Street, Suite 210 • Honolulu, Hawaiʻi 96816
Ph: (808) 732-1709 • Fax: (808) 734-4094
www.mutualpublishing.com
e-mail: mutual@mutualpublishing.com

Printed in Korea

# INTRODUCTION

by U'i Goldsberry

A sway of hips, flutter of fingers, a gentle smile, and the flowing movements of the *hela* and *ami* are all parts of the hula. The romance and grace of this uniquely Hawaiian art form has captured the imagination of the world. Once reviled by those who came to the Islands to preach of a Christian god, the hula has adapted and blossomed into a living entity that breathes life into the souls of Hawai'i's people.

From its origins in the bosom of the god Laka, to extravagant modern-day festivals, the hula transcends time and presents Hawai'i's ancient culture in a visual celebration of physical glory. It blesses all who have the privilege of participating in the dance.

*Hula,* a book filled with proverbs, quotes, and stunning images, honors the masters of the dance, those *kumu hula* who study the ancient *mele* and teach their *haumana* the *kauna* of their ancestors. *Kuhi no ka lima, hele no ka maka*—where the hands move, let the eyes follow. The eyes must be watchful while the hands create the future.

"The hula is Hawai'i. The hula is the history of our country. The hula is a story itself if it's done right. And the hula, to me, is the foundation of life. It teaches us how to live, how to be, is the ability to create one's inner feelings and no one else's."

– George Nā'ope

"At night they feasted and the girls danced the lascivious hula-hula— a dance that is said to exhibit the very perfection of educated motion of limb and arm, hand, head and body, and the exactest uniformity of movement and accuracy of 'time.' It was performed by a circle of girls with no raiment on them to speak of, who went through an infinite variety of motions and figures without prompting, and yet so true was their 'time,' and in such perfect concert did they move that when they were placed in a straight line, hands, arms, bodies, limbs, and heads waved, swayed, gesticulated, bowed, stooped, whirled, squirmed, twisted, and undulated as if they were part and parcel of a single individual; and it was difficult to believe they were not moved in a body of some exquisite piece of mechanism."

— Mark Twain

## I leʻa ka hula i ka hoʻopaʻa.

### The hula is pleasing because of the drummer.

The lesser details that one pays little attention to are just as important as the major ones. Although the attention is given to the dancer, the drummer and chanter play an important role in the dance.

Hawaiian hula eyes
When you dance you hypnotize
Though I can't believe it's true

Hawaiian hula eyes
It's you I'm dreaming of
With a haunting dream of love

On the sands of Lunga Bay
Where the sighing zephyrs play
I'm reminded of the one I love

Beneath the swaying palms
I held you in my arms
My Hawaiian hula eyes

– William Harbottle and Randy Oness,
"Hawaiian Hula Eyes"

Aloha Nui
FROM
Hawaiian
Islands.

## Hōpoe, ka wahine lewa i ke kai.

### Hōpoe, the woman who dances in the sea.

Hōpoe was a dancer of Kea'au, Puna, in that long ago day when gods mingled with men. Because of her dancing and her kindly nature, Hōpoe was taken by the goddess Hi'iaka as a favorite friend. When Pele sent Hi'iaka to Kaua'i to fetch Lohi'au, the first request Hi'iaka made to Pele was to be kind to her friend, Hōpoe. After a time, when Hi'iaka did not return as expected, Pele in a fit of rage destroyed Hi'iaka's grove and the beloved Hōpoe. The latter was changing into a balancing stone that seemed to dance in the sea.

"Traditions are like an unbroken piece of thread. It connects every era."

– Pōhaku Nishimitsu

**Kuhi no ka lima,**
**hele no ka maka.**

Where the hands move,
there let the eyes follow.

A rule in hula.

"The hālau hula...schools teach more than dance...at the same time (they) help to preserve the language and some of the myths, rituals, and customs of the past. Their impact is significant because of the large number of people who are involved as teachers, students, and audiences. In some hālau where the kumu hula are particularly strict with their discipline, the impact on the students is profound and life-long."

– George Kanahele

"Hula is the art of Hawaiian dance expressing all we see, hear, smell, taste, touch and feel."

– Maiki Aiu

**Mai pa'a i ka leo,
he 'ole ka hea mai.**

Do not withhold the voice and
not call out [a welcome].

From a password chant used in hula schools.
It was often used by one who would like a
friendly invitation to come into another's home.

## "Dance we will—no tabu!"

– Governor Boki of O'ahu
(responding to a missionary's
repeated request that dancing
at a royal funeral be banned)

**"We as students can learn from our kumu hula and duplicate their teaching or their style of dance. When it comes to expressing ourselves, our expression comes from within ourselves."**

– Odetta Kaohikukapulani Kinimaka-Alquiza

**Pa'i ana nā pahu a hula le'a;**
**'o ka'u hula nō kēia.**

Let the better-enjoyed hula chanters beat their own drums; this is the hula chant that I know.

A retort: Let those who claim to know a lot produce their knowledge; this is what I know.

"(Through the hula) we are endowed with a great heritage."

– Maiki Aiu

"The hula was a religious service in which poetry, music, pantomime, and the dance lent themselves, under the form of dramatic art, to the refreshment of men's minds. Its view of life was idyllic, it gave itself to the celebration of those mythical times when gods and goddesses moved on the earth, and men and women were as gods."

– Nathaniel Emerson

**'A'a i ka hula, waiho**
**ka hilahila i ka hale.**

When one wants to dance the hula,
bashfulness should be left at home.

Also expressed A'o i ka hula,...

Hula Dancer, Hawaiian Islands.

H - 288 Hilo Hattie
KODA
HAWA
LTD

"The hula is a descriptive dance. It's lovely. And we tell you a story. And we describe the story with our hands. The rest of the movements are added to make it more graceful. So we tell you to 'keep your eyes on the hands.' I catch more guys watching the wrong places all the time."

– Clara Haili, known to the world as "Hilo Hattie"

"The Hawaiian hula has been, over the years, probably the best known and least understood of the fine arts in Hawai'i. First, the missionaries condemned it to hell fire. Then tin-pan alley turned it into a dance no self-respecting Hawaiian would perform. But the hula has survived these indignities to remain the heartbeat of Hawai'i."

– Bob Krauss

**"Hula teaches you everything about life. It teaches you about nature, respect, and about God."**

– Kamalei Sataraka

**"As a dancer you're painting a picture. You put into motion our oral history."**

– Cecilia Kawaiokawa'awa'a Akim

"The easiest way to memorize our history is by doing it through the hula. Hula keeps our history and our people alive, and without it one cannot truly identify oneself as being Hawaiian."

– Al Makahinu Barcarse

**Hōʻaleʻale Mānā i ke kaha o Kaunalewa.**

Mānā ripples over the land of Kaunalewa.

Said of movements of a dance.
A play on ʻaleʻale (to ripple like water), referring to the hands, and lewa (to sway), referring to the movement of the hips.

**"I love a pretty little**
**Honolulu hula hula girl,**
**She's the candy kid to wriggle,**
**Hula girl,**
**She will surely make you giggle,**
**Hula girl,**
**With her naughty little wiggle..."**

– Albert R. "Sonny" Cunha,
*"Honolulu Hula Girl"*

**"They strike their hands on the pit of their stomach smartly and jump all together, at the same time repeating the words of a song in response."**

– David Samwell, Captain of Captain Cook's ship, *Discovery* (1778)

**Niniu Molokaʻi, poahi Lānaʻi.**

Molokaʻi revolves, Lānaʻi sways.

A description of the revolving of the hips and the swaying movements in hula.

"...a student's knowledge...of the hula should be ever-maturing—deepening and broadening..."

– Maiki Aiu

"Let your feelings show in your face. Everything you feel, must show in your whole being. If you're doing a hula about a person, you must study the person so well that you feel you know them. Your feelings must show through so well in everything you do as you dance, that the audience feels it has experienced the presence of the person you are dancing about. It is the same when you dance about things of nature. You must have aloha for it, understand it, before you can dance it."

– Helen Desha Beamer

**ʻUnu mai a hoʻonuʻanuʻa ke kilu o Kalamaʻula, hoʻoleʻaleʻa i ke kaha o Kaunalewa.**

Bring all the kilu for amusement at Kamalaʻula to make merry on the field of Kaunalewa.

To come together for a gay time and bring whatever you have to add to the fun. There is a play on lewa, which refers to the swinging of the hips in hula.

"...it was performed two at a time. They did not jump up as in the common dance but used a kind of regular step and moved their legs something like our sailors dancing a Hornpipe, they moved their arms up and down, repeated a song together, changed their places often, wiggled their backsides and used many lascivious gestures. Upon the whole we thought it much more agreeable than their common dance."

– David Samwell, Captain of Captain Cook's ship, *Discovery* (1778)

My first years of hula focused on
the feet. From August to April basic
steps were taught. The steps were to
be mastered before any other learning.
It was quite like building a house...
Hand movements would follow.
Hula practice was a constant repetition.
It was a time of learning and realization.
One might say that the awareness of
the physical, emotional, and mental
bodies is heightened through hula.

– Lehua Huliha'e, Kumu hula

**E hea i ke kanaka e komo maloko e hānai ai a hewa ke waha.**

Call to the person to enter;
feed him until he can take no more.

Originally a reply to a password into a hula school. Used later in songs and in speech to extend hospitality.

# References


Ariyoshi, Rita. *Hula is Life: The Story of Hālau Hula O Maiki.* Honolulu: Maiki Aiu Building Corporation, 1998.

Davis, Lynn Ann. "Photographically Illustrated Books about Hawai'i, 1854–1945." *The Hawaiian Journal of History, Volume 35, 2001.* Honolulu: Hawaiian Historical Society, 2001.

Emerson, Nathaniel B. *Unwritten Literature of Hawai'i.* Honolulu: Mutual Publishing, 1998.

Harden, M. J. *Voices of Wisdom: Hawaiian Elders Speak.* Aka Press, 1999.

Hopkins, Jerry. *The Hula.* Hong Kong: Apa Productions, 1982.

Itagaki, Jan M. and Lependdu, Lovina, eds. *Nānā I Nā Loea Hula: Look to the Hula Resources.* Honolulu: Kalihi-Palama Culture & Arts Society, Inc., 1997.

Kanahele, George. *Ku Kanaka: Stand Tall.* Honolulu: University of Hawai'i Press, 1986.

Pukui, Mary Kawena. *'Ōlelo No'eau: Hawaiian Proverbs & Poetical Sayings.* Honolulu: Bishop Museum Special Publication No. 71, 1983.

Ronck, Ronn. *Celebration: A Portrait of Hawai'i Through the Songs of the Brothers Cazimero.* Honolulu: Mutual Publishing, 1984.

Samwell, David. *A Narrative of the Death of Captain James Cook.* London: 1786.

# Photo Credits

Page 2: old postcard image
Page 5: old postcard image
Pages 6-7: old postcard image
Page 8: Bishop Museum
Page 9: old postcard image
Page 10: Francis Haar
Page 11: Boone Morrison
Page 12: Hawai'i State Archives
Page 14: Bishop Museum
Page 17: Francis Haar
Page 19: old postcard image
Page 20: old postcard image
Page 22: Hedemann Collection, Bishop Museum
Page 25: old postcard image
Page 27: Bishop Museum
Pages 28-29: Walter M. Giffard, Bishop Museum
Page 30: Hawai'i State Archives
Page 32: old postcard image
Page 35: Bishop Museum
Page 37: Bishop Museum
Page 38: Bishop Museum
Page 40: old postcard image
Page 43: Hawai'i State Archives
Page 45: old postcard image
Page 46: old postcard image
Page 48: old postcard image
Page 51: Bishop Museum
Page 53: Francis Haar
Pages 54-55: old postcard image
Page 56: Francis Haar
Page 58: Hawaiian Mission Children's Society
Page 61: old postcard image
Page 63: Boone Morrison
Page 64: W. T. Brigham Collection, Bishop Museum
Page 66: Baker-Van Dyke Collection, Bishop Museum
Page 69: Hawai'i Visitors Bureau
Page 71: old postcard image
Page 72: Bishop Museum
Page 74: Hawai'i State Archives
Page 77: Hawai'i State Archives
Page 80: Hawai'i State Archives